26
Bahá'í
Prayers

Revealed by 'Abdu'l-Bahá

First published in March 2021

a
gift
from
the
heart

'ABDU'L-BAHÁ

In the early years of the 20th century, 'Abdu'l-Bahá—the eldest Son of Bahá'u'lláh—was the Bahá'í Faith's leading exponent, renowned as a champion of social justice and an ambassador for international peace.

'Abdu'l-Bahá devoted His ministry to furthering His Father's Faith and to promoting the ideals of peace and unity. He encouraged the establishment of local Bahá'í institutions, and guided nascent educational, social and economic initiatives. After His release from a lifetime of imprisonment, 'Abdu'l-Bahá set out on a series of journeys which took Him to Egypt, Europe and North America. Throughout His life, He presented with brilliant simplicity, to high and low alike, Bahá'u'lláh's prescription for the spiritual and social renewal of society.

HE IS GOD.

O thou who circlest in adoration about the Spot round which circle the Concourse on high! Raise thou thy hands in gratitude at the Threshold of the one true God, and say: O Thou the highest aspiration of every ardent lover! O Thou the Guide of every wandering soul! Thou hast favoured this feeble servant with Thine infinite blessings, and led this hapless and lowly one unto the Threshold of Thy oneness. Thou hast lifted to these parched lips the living waters of Thy loving-kindness and revived this weary and withered soul with the breezes of divine mercy. I yield Thee thanks for having bestowed upon me a full portion from Thy most gracious favour and invested me with the honour of attaining unto Thy sacred Threshold.[1]
I beseech an infinite share from the bounties of Thy Kingdom on high. Grant Thine assistance. Confer Thy gracious favour.

'Abdu'l-Bahá

[1] *Reference to the Shrine of The Báb*

O THOU UNSEEN FRIEND!

O Desire of all in this world and the world to come!
O Thou compassionate Beloved! These helpless
souls are captivated by Thy love, and these feeble
ones seek shelter at Thy Threshold. Every night
they sigh and moan in their remoteness from Thee,
and every morn they lament and weep by reason
of the onslaught of the people of malice. They are
afflicted at every moment with a fresh anguish,
and are sore tried at each breath by the tyranny
of every wicked oppressor. Praise be to Thee that,
notwithstanding this, they are ablaze as a temple
of fire and shine resplendent as the sun and the
moon. They stand tall, like upraised banners,
in the Cause of God, and hasten, like valiant
horsemen, into the arena. They have bloomed like
sweet blossoms and are filled with joy like the
laughing rose. Wherefore, O Thou loving Provider,
graciously assist these holy souls by Thy heavenly
grace which is vouchsafed from Thy Kingdom, and
grant that these sanctified beings may manifest the
signs of the Most High. Thou art the All-Bountiful,
the Pitiful, the All-Merciful, the Compassionate.

'Abdu'l-Bahá

O THOU PEERLESS
AND LOVING LORD!

Though capacity and worthiness are lacking, and it is infinitely hard to withstand tribulations, yet worthiness and capacity are gifts vouchsafed by Thee. O Lord! Give us capacity and make us worthy, that we may evince the most great steadfastness, renounce this world and all its people, kindle the fire of Thy love, and even as candles, burn bright with a consuming flame and shed abroad our radiance.

O Lord of the Kingdom! Deliver us from this world of vain illusions, and lead us unto the realm of the infinite. Suffer us to be wholly freed from this nether life, and cause us to be blessed with the bountiful gifts of the Kingdom. Release us from this world of nothingness that beareth the semblance of reality, and confer upon us life everlasting. Bestow on us joy and delight, and favour us with gladness and contentment. Comfort our hearts, and grant peace and tranquillity to our souls, so that upon ascending unto Thy Kingdom we may attain Thy presence and may rejoice in the realms above. Thou art the Giver, the Bestower, the Almighty!

'Abdu'l-Bahá

O MY ETERNAL BELOVED AND MY ADORED FRIEND!

How long shall I remain bereft of Thy presence and sorely afflicted by remoteness from Thee? To the retreats of Thy heavenly Kingdom lead me, and at the scene of the appearance of Thy supernal Realm cast upon me the glance of Thy loving- kindness.

O Thou Omnipotent Lord! Number me among the denizens of the Kingdom. This mortal world is my abode; grant me a habitation in the realms of the Placeless. To this earthly plane I pertain; shed upon me the effulgence of Thy glorious light. In this world of dust I dwell; make me an inmate of Thy heavenly realm, so that I may lay down my life in Thy path and attain to my heart's desire, may crown my head with the diadem of divine favour and raise the triumphal cry of "O Glory of God, the Most Glorious!"

'Abdu'l-Bahá

O THOU KIND LORD!

These souls are Thy friends who are gathered together and are carried away by Thy love. They are transported by the rays of Thy beauty and captivated by Thy musk- laden locks. They have surrendered their hearts to Thee and, lowly and helpless, wander in Thy path. They have forsaken friend and stranger alike and have laid hold of Thy unity, bowing in adoration before Thee.

They belonged to this nether world; Thou didst welcome them into Thy Kingdom. They were as withered plants in the wilderness of deprivation and loss; Thou didst make them the saplings of the garden of knowledge and understanding. Their voices were stilled; Thou didst cause them to speak forth. They were dispirited; Thou didst shed illumination upon them. They were as parched and barren soil; Thou didst turn them into a rose-garden of inner meanings. They were as children in the world of humanity; Thou didst enable them to attain heavenly maturity.

O Thou kind One! Grant them a haven and a refuge within the shelter of Thy protection, and shield them from tests and trials. Lend them Thine invisible assistance, and confer upon them Thine infallible grace.

O Thou kind and beloved Lord! They are as the body, and Thou art the Spirit of life. The body is dependent for its freshness and beauty upon the grace of the spirit. They stand, therefore, in need of Thy confirmations and yearn for the sustaining power of the Holy Spirit in this new Revelation. Thou art the Mighty. Thou art the Giver, the Provider, the Bestower, and the Forgiver. Thou art the One Who shineth brightly from the invisible Realm.

'Abdu'l-Bahá

O DIVINE PROVIDENCE!

Perplexing difficulties have arisen and formidable obstacles have appeared. O Lord! Remove these difficulties and show forth the evidences of Thy might and power. Ease these hardships and smooth our way along this arduous path. O Divine Providence! The obstacles are unyielding, and our toil and hardship are conjoined with a myriad adversities. There is no helper save Thee, and no succourer except Thyself. We set all our hopes on Thee, and commit all our affairs unto Thy care. Thou art the Guide and the Remover of every difficulty, and Thou art the Wise, the Seeing, and the Hearing.

'Abdu'l-Bahá

O GOD OF MERCY!

O Thou Omnipotent One! I am but a feeble servant, weak and helpless, but I have been nurtured within the shelter of Thy grace and favour, nourished from the breast of Thy mercy, and reared in the bosom of Thy loving-kindness. O Lord! Poor and needy though I be, yet every needy one is made prosperous through Thy bounty, while every wealthy one, if bereft of Thy favours, is indeed poor and desolate.

O Divine Providence! Grant me the strength to bear this heavy burden, and enable me to safeguard this supreme bestowal, for so strong is the force of tests and so grievous the onslaught of trials that every mountain is scattered in dust, and the highest peak reduced to nothing. Thou knowest full well that in my heart I seek naught but Thy remembrance, and in my soul I desire nothing save Thy love. Raise me up to serve Thy loved ones, and let me abide forever in servitude at Thy Threshold. Thou art the Loving. Thou art the Lord of manifold bounties.

'Abdu'l-Bahá

O DIVINE PROVIDENCE!

Awaken me and make me conscious. Cause me to be detached from all else save Thee, and captivate me by the love of Thy beauty. Waft upon me the breath of the Holy Spirit, and suffer me to hearken to the call of the Abhá Kingdom. Bestow upon me heavenly power, and kindle the lamp of the spirit within the innermost chamber of my heart. Release me from every bond, and deliver me from every attachment, that I may cherish no desire except Thy good-pleasure, seek naught besides Thy Countenance, and tread no path other than Thy path. Grant that I may enable the heedless to become mindful and the slumberers to awaken, that I may proffer the water of life to those who are sore athirst and bring divine healing to those who are sick and ailing.

Though I am lowly, abased, and poor, yet Thou art my haven and my refuge, my supporter and my helper. Send down Thine aid in such wise that all may be astounded. O God! Thou art, verily, the Almighty, the Most Powerful, the Giver, the Bestower, and the All-Seeing.

'Abdu'l-Bahá

HE IS GOD.

O God, my God! I have set my face towards Thee, and supplicate the outpourings of the ocean of Thy healing. Graciously assist me, O Lord, to serve Thy people and to heal Thy servants. If Thou dost aid me, the remedy I offer will become a healing medicine for every ailment, a draught of life-giving waters for every burning thirst, and a soothing balm for every yearning heart. If Thou dost not aid me, it will be naught but affliction itself, and I will scarcely bring healing to any soul.

O God, my God! Aid and assist me through Thy power to heal the sick. Thou art, verily, the Healer, the Sufficer, He Who is the remover of every pain and sickness, He Who hath dominion over all things.

'Abdu'l-Bahá

O LORD!

Grant me a measure of Thy grace and loving-kindness, Thy care and protection, Thy shelter and bounty, that the end of my days may be distinguished above their beginning, and the close of my life may open the portals to Thy manifold blessings. May Thy loving-kindness and bounty descend upon me at every moment, and Thy forgiveness and mercy be vouchsafed with every breath, until, beneath the sheltering shadow of Thine upraised Standard, I may at last repair to the Kingdom of the All-Praised. Thou art the Bestower and the Ever-Loving, and Thou art, verily, the Lord of grace and bounty.

'Abdu'l-Bahá

O THOU PROVIDER, O THOU FORGIVER!

A noble soul hath ascended unto the Kingdom of reality, and hastened from the mortal world of dust to the realm of everlasting glory. Exalt the station of this recently arrived guest, and attire this long-standing servant with a new and wondrous robe.

O Thou Peerless Lord! Grant Thy forgiveness and tender care so that this soul may be admitted into the retreats of Thy mysteries and may become an intimate companion in the assemblage of splendours. Thou art the Giver, the Bestower, the Ever-Loving. Thou art the Pardoner, the Tender, the Most Powerful.

'Abdu'l-Bahá

HE IS GOD.

O Thou forgiving Lord! These servants were noble souls, and these radiant hearts were made illumined and resplendent through the light of Thy guidance. They drank a brimming cup of the wine of Thy love, and gave ear to eternal mysteries imparted by the melodies of Thy knowledge. They bound their hearts to Thee, broke free from the snare of estrangement, and laid hold of Thy unity. Make these precious souls companions of the inmates of Heaven, and admit them into the circle of Thy chosen ones. Make them intimates of Thy mysteries in the retreats of the realm above, and immerse them in the sea of lights. Thou art the Bestower, the Luminous, and the Kind.

'Abdu'l-Bahá

O DIVINE PROVIDENCE!

Immerse the father and mother of this servant of Thy Threshold in the ocean of Thy forgiveness, and purge and sanctify them from every sin and transgression. Grant them Thy forgiveness and mercy, and bestow upon them Thy gracious pardon. Thou, verily, art the Pardoner, the Ever-Forgiving, the Bestower of abundant grace. O Thou forgiving Lord! Though we are sinners, yet our hopes are fixed upon Thy promise and assurance. Though we are enveloped by the darkness of error, yet we have at all times turned our faces to the morn of Thy bountiful favours. Deal with us as beseemeth Thy Threshold, and confer upon us that which is worthy of Thy Court. Thou art the Ever-Forgiving, the Pardoner, He Who overlooketh every shortcoming.

'Abdu'l-Bahá

O THOU KIND LORD!

Sanctify my heart from all attachment, and gladden my soul with tidings of joy. Free me from attachment to friend and stranger alike, and captivate me with Thy love, that I may become wholly devoted to Thee and be filled with fervid rapture; that I may desire naught but Thee, seek no one except Thyself, tread no other path besides Thine, and commune only with Thee; that I may, even as a nightingale, be spellbound by Thy love and, by day and night, sigh and wail and weep and cry out, "Yá Bahá'u'l-Abhá!"

'Abdu'l-Bahá

O LORD!

What an outpouring of bounty Thou hast vouchsafed, and what a flood of abounding grace Thou hast granted! Thou didst make all the hearts to become even as a single heart, and all the souls to be bound together as one soul. Thou didst endow inert bodies with life and feeling, and didst bestow upon lifeless frames the consciousness of the spirit. Through the effulgent rays shed from the Day-Star of the All-Merciful, Thou didst invest these atoms of dust with visible existence, and through the billows of the ocean of oneness, Thou didst enable these evanescent drops to surge and roar.

O Almighty One Who endowest a blade of straw with the might of a mountain and enablest a speck of dust to mirror forth the glory of the resplendent sun! Grant us Thy tender grace and favour, so that we may arise to serve Thy Cause and not be shamefaced before the peoples of the earth.

'Abdu'l-Bahá

O THOU OMNIPOTENT LORD!

We are all held within the mighty grasp of Thy power. Thou art our Supporter and our Helper. Grant us Thy tender mercy, bestow upon us Thy bounty, open the portals of grace, and cast upon us the glance of Thy favours. Let a vivifying breeze waft over us, and quicken Thou our yearning hearts. Illumine our eyes and make the sanctuary of our hearts the envy of every blossoming bower. Rejoice every soul and gladden every spirit. Reveal Thine ancient power and make manifest Thy great might. Cause the birds of human souls to soar to new heights, and let Thy confidants in this nether world fathom the mysteries of Thy Kingdom. Set firm our steps and bestow upon us unwavering hearts. We are sinners, and Thou art the Ever-Forgiving. We are Thy servants, and Thou art the Sovereign Lord. We are homeless wanderers, and Thou art our haven and refuge. Graciously aid and assist us to diffuse Thy sweet savours and

to exalt Thy Word. Elevate the station of the dispossessed, and bestow Thine inexhaustible treasure upon the destitute. Vouchsafe Thy strength unto the weak, and confer heavenly power upon the feeble. Thou art the Provider, Thou art the Gracious, Thou art the Lord Who ruleth over all things.

'Abdu'l-Bahá

HE IS THE MOST HOLY, THE MOST GLORIOUS.

In the name of God, the Compassionate, the Merciful! Praise be to God, the Lord of all worlds!

O Lord my God, my Haven and my Refuge! How can I befittingly make mention of Thee, even with the most wondrous words of glorification or the most eloquent odes of praise, O Thou Almighty and Forgiving One, aware as I am that the tongue of every eloquent speaker doth falter, and every expression of praise from either human pen or tongue is confounded in its attempt to glorify but one of the signs of Thine omnipotent power or to extol a single Word that hath been created by Thee. Indeed, the wings of the birds of human minds are broken in their attempt to soar up to the atmosphere of Thy divine holiness, and the spiders of idle fancy are powerless to weave their frail webs upon the loftiest summits of the canopy of Thy knowledge. No recourse is there for me, then, but to acknowledge my powerlessness and shortcomings, and no habitation is there for me but in the depths of poverty and privation. Verily, powerlessness to comprehend Thee is the essence of understanding, confession of shortcomings is the only means of attaining Thy presence, and admission of poverty is the source of true wealth.

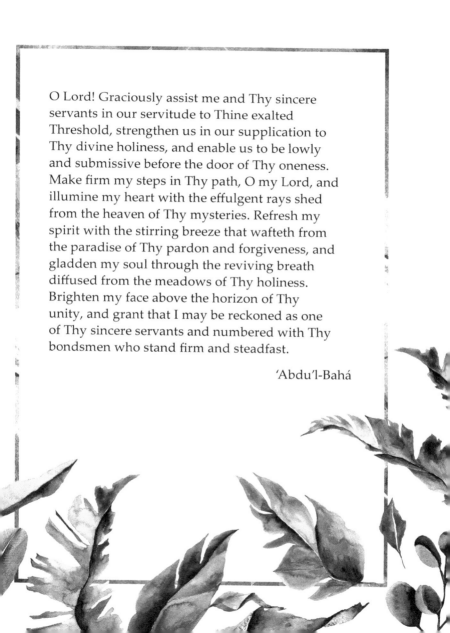

O Lord! Graciously assist me and Thy sincere servants in our servitude to Thine exalted Threshold, strengthen us in our supplication to Thy divine holiness, and enable us to be lowly and submissive before the door of Thy oneness. Make firm my steps in Thy path, O my Lord, and illumine my heart with the effulgent rays shed from the heaven of Thy mysteries. Refresh my spirit with the stirring breeze that wafteth from the paradise of Thy pardon and forgiveness, and gladden my soul through the reviving breath diffused from the meadows of Thy holiness. Brighten my face above the horizon of Thy unity, and grant that I may be reckoned as one of Thy sincere servants and numbered with Thy bondsmen who stand firm and steadfast.

'Abdu'l-Bahá

O LORD, OUR GOD!

We are helpless; Thou art the Lord of strength and power. We are wretched; Thou art the Almighty, the All-Glorious. We are poor; Thou art the All-Possessing, the Most Generous. Graciously assist us in our servitude to Thy sacred Threshold, and aid us, through Thy strengthening grace, to worship Thee at the dawning-places of Thy praise. Enable us to diffuse Thy holy fragrances amongst Thy creatures, and strengthen our loins to serve Thee amidst Thy servants, so that we may guide all nations to Thy Most Great Name and lead all peoples to the shores of the glorious ocean of Thy oneness.

O Lord! Deliver us from the attachments of the world and its peoples, from the transgressions of the past, and from the afflictions yet to come, that we may arise to exalt Thy Word with the utmost joy and radiance and celebrate Thy praise in the daytime and in the night season, that we may summon all people to the way of guidance and enjoin them to observe righteousness, and that we may chant the verses of Thy unity amidst all Thy creation. Potent art Thou to do what pleaseth Thee. Thou art, verily, the Almighty, the Most Powerful.

'Abdu'l-Bahá

HE IS GOD.

O Thou kind and beloved Lord! These friends are exhilarated with the wine of the Covenant and are wanderers in the wilderness of Thy love. Their hearts are consumed by the flames of

remoteness from Thee, and they yearn eagerly for the revelation of Thy splendours. From Thine invisible Kingdom, the Realm of the unseen, reveal unto them the effulgent glory of Thy grace, and shed upon them the radiance of Thy bounty. At every moment, send forth a new blessing and reveal a fresh favour.

O Divine Providence! We are weak and Thou art the Most Powerful. We are as tiny ants and Thou art the King of the Realm of Glory. Bestow Thy grace and confer Thy bounty upon us, that we may kindle a flame and shed its splendour abroad, that we may show forth strength and render some service. Grant that we may bring illumination to this darksome earth and spirituality to this fleeting world of dust. Suffer us not to rest for a moment, nor to defile ourselves with the transitory things of this life. Enable us to prepare a banquet of guidance, inscribe with our life- blood the verses of love, leave fear and peril behind, become even as fruitful trees, and cause human perfections to

appear in this ephemeral world. Thou, in truth, art the All-Bountiful, the Most Compassionate, the Ever-Forgiving, the Pardoner.

'Abdu'l-Bahá

HE IS THE ALL-GLORIOUS.

O my Lord, my King, my Ruler, and my Sovereign!
I call upon Thee with my tongue, my heart, and
my soul, saying: Clothe this servant of Thine with
the robe of Thy care, the raiment of Thine unfailing
help, and the armour of Thy protection. Assist him
to make mention of Thee and to extol Thy virtues
amidst Thy people, and unloose his tongue to utter
Thy glorification and praise in every assemblage
held to celebrate Thy unity and sanctity. Thou
art, in truth, the Mighty, the Powerful, the All-
Glorious, the Self-Subsisting.

'Abdu'l-Bahá

O MY KIND LORD, O THOU THE DESIRE OF MY HEART AND SOUL!

Bestow upon Thy friends Thy loving-kindness, and grant them Thine unfailing mercy. Be Thou a solace to Thine ardent lovers, and a friend, a comforter, and a loving companion to them who yearn for Thee. Their hearts are ablaze with the fire of Thy love, and their souls are consumed with the flame of devotion to Thee. They long, one and all, to hasten unto the altar of love, that they may willingly lay down their lives.

O Divine Providence! Grant them Thy favour, guide them aright, graciously aid them to achieve spiritual victory, and confer upon them heavenly bestowals. O Lord, assist them by Thy munificence and grace, and make their radiant faces lamps of guidance in assemblies devoted to the knowledge of Thee, and signs of heavenly bounty in gatherings where Thy verses are expounded. Thou art, verily, the Merciful, the All-Bountiful, the One Whose help is implored by all men.

'Abdu'l-Bahá

HE IS THE ALL-GLORIOUS,
THE MOST EFFULGENT.

O Divine Providence, O forgiving Lord! How can I ever befittingly sing Thy praise or sufficiently worship and glorify Thee? Thy description by any tongue is naught but error, and Thy depiction by any pen is an evidence of folly in attempting this formidable task. The tongue is but an instrument composed of elements; voice and speech are naught but accidental attributes. How, then, can I celebrate, with the instrument of an earthly voice, the praise of Him Who hath neither peer nor likeness? All that I can say or seek is limited by the grasp of the human mind and encompassed by the bounds of the human world. How can human thought ever scale the lofty summits of divine holiness, and how can the spider of idle fancy ever weave the frail web of vain imaginings upon the retreats of sanctity? Naught can I do but testify to my powerlessness and confess my failure. Thou art, verily, He Who is the All-Possessing, the Inaccessible, He Who is immeasurably exalted above the comprehension of them that are endued with understanding.

'Abdu'l-Bahá

O DIVINE PROVIDENCE, THOU ART THE EVER-FORGIVING!

O Thou Almighty God, Thou art the Gracious! Let this dearly loved servant of Thine abide beneath the shadow of Thy glory, and grant that this hapless and lowly one may prosper and flourish within the precincts of Thy mercy. Give him to drink from the chalice of Thy nearness, and let him abide under the shade of the Blessed Tree. Confer upon him the honour of attaining Thy presence, and bestow upon him everlasting bliss. Graciously assist the surviving kindred of this noble soul to follow in the footsteps of their dear father, to show forth his character and conduct amongst all people, to follow Thy path, seek Thy good-pleasure, and utter Thy praise. Thou art the Ever-Loving God, the Lord of bounty.

'Abdu'l-Bahá

O THOU INCOMPARABLE GOD!

We are Thy humble servants, and Thou art the All-Glorious. We are sinners, and Thou art the Ever-Forgiving. We are captives, poor and lowly, and Thou art our shelter and our aid. We are as tiny ants, and Thou art the Lord of majesty, enthroned in the highest heaven. Protect us, as a token of Thy grace, and withhold not from us Thy care and assistance. O Lord! Thy tests are indeed severe, and Thy trials can lay in ruin foundations wrought of steel. Preserve and strengthen us; cheer and gladden our hearts. Graciously assist us to serve, even as 'Abdu'l-Bahá, Thy sacred Threshold.

'Abdu'l-Bahá

HE IS GOD.

O God, my God! With utter lowliness and fervour, humility and devotion, I implore Thee with my tongue and my heart, with my spirit and my soul, and with my mind and my conscience, to grant the most cherished of all desires, destine the most meritorious of all deeds, and ordain all honour and perfection, favour and beauty, prosperity and salvation for this family that hath hastened to Thy sheltering shadow at the break of Thy resplendent morn and sought refuge within Thy safe haven and Thy mighty stronghold. Verily, these souls heeded Thy call, drew nigh unto Thy Threshold, were set aflame with the fire of Thy love, and were carried away by the breaths of Thy holiness. They were constant in the service of Thy Cause, humble before Thy Countenance, and noble beneath Thy sheltering shadow. They are renowned as the bearers of Thy name amongst Thy people and make mention of Thee amidst Thy servants.

O God, my God! Exalt them by Thine ancient glory, honour them in Thy Kingdom of grandeur, and assist them with the hosts of Thy favours in this great Day. O Lord, my God! Raise aloft their banner, grant them an ampler share of Thy protection, spread abroad their signs, and increase their radiance, that they may become a glass for the lamp of Thy manifold favours and spreaders of Thy loving-kindness and bounties.

O Lord, my God! Be Thou their companion in their loneliness, and in their moments of anguish surround them with Thine aid. Bequeath unto them Thy Book and vouchsafe unto them the full measure of Thy gifts and bestowals. Thou art in truth the Mighty, the Powerful, the Gracious, the Bountiful, and verily, Thou art the Merciful, the Compassionate.

'Abdu'l-Bahá

O LORD SO RICH IN BOUNTY, SO
REPLETE WITH GRACE, WHOSE
KNOWLEDGE DOTH MINE INMOST
HEART AND SOUL EMBRACE!

At morn, the solace of my soul is none but Thee;
The knower of my loss and woe is none but Thee.

The heart that for a moment hath Thy mention known
Will seek no friend save longing pain for Thee alone.

Withered be the heart that sigheth not for Thee,
And better blind the eye that crieth not for Thee!

In all mine hours of deepest gloom, O Lord of might,
My heart hath Thy remembrance for a shining light.

Do, through Thy favour, breathe Thy spirit into me,
That what hath never been may thus forever be.

Consider not our merit and our worth,
O Lord of bounty, but the grace Thou pourest forth.

Upon these broken-winged birds whose flight is slow
Out of Thy tender mercy newfound wings bestow.

'Abdu'l-Bahá

CPSIA information can be obtained
at www.ICGtesting.com
Printed in the USA
BVHW090126221221
624588BV00011B/974

9 781922 562456